OXFORD

THE COLLEGES
AND UNIVERSITY

First published 2004 by
Chris Andrews Publications Ltd, Oxford
Updated and reprinted 2011
Photographed and produced by Chris Andrews
Text David Huelin
Design Mike Brain

All material © Chris Andrews
www.cap-ox.com

ISBN 978 1 9067255 8 7

For copies of this book with your company logo and corporate
message or for picture library requests please contact
Chris Andrews Publications Ltd

Front cover Merton College and Oxford
Back cover Punting at Magdalen Bridge
Endpapers Ceiling detail Duke Humfrey's Library
Title page The Chancellor's Throne in The Sheldonian Theatre

ACKNOWLEDGEMENT

Many thanks to the Colleges and University of Oxford for their
encouragement and kind permission to show their many aspects.
Christ Church by permission of the Governing Body of Christ
Church, Oxford. The inclusion of a building or view in this work
does not necessarily indicate a right of public access.

Originated and printed by Butler Tanner and Dennis Ltd
Frome and London

CHRIS ANDREWS PUBLICATIONS LTD
15 Curtis Yard, North Hinksey Lane
Oxford OX2 0LX

Telephone: +44(0)1865 723404
Email: chris.andrews1@btclick.com
www.cap-ox.com

OXFORD
THE COLLEGES
AND UNIVERSITY

CHRIS ANDREWS PUBLICATIONS LTD

CONTENTS

FOREWORD

THE RT HON THE LORD PATTEN OF BARNES, CH
CHANCELLOR OF THE UNIVERSITY OF OXFORD

Oxford is one of the greatest cities in Europe. One of the foundation stones of Western Civilisation, it has been for centuries a great centre of scholarship, pushing back the frontiers of knowledge. Oxford has made history and been shaped in its turn by the history of our continent and of our own country.

Inevitably, Oxford has been painted, photographed and written about, again and again, and this book shows why. The city contains some of the greatest prizes of our architectural heritage, handsome and elegant buildings that mark the development of our culture. But it contains hidden charms as well as stately magnificence, and part of the attraction of this book is that it conveys so well the atmosphere of this remarkable city.

INTRODUCTION

Oxford has been the home of England's oldest university since before the year 1200. There were then three monastic schools with some tradition of learning, and when in 1167 the English scholars at the University of Paris were obliged to leave, King Henry II persuaded many of them to come to Oxford. They brought their experience of the ancient curriculum of studies in force at Paris and they set up a similar course in Oxford.

The system was based on a guild of Masters to which scholars, after seven years' studies in the liberal arts, would be admitted with a licence to teach, and some obligation to do so. All teaching was under the Church (of Rome) and all scholars, Masters, and Doctors were in holy orders, tonsured, and wearing a long black gown.

The scholars were of humble parentage; in an age when the nobility were illiterate and there were no middle classes, the administration of Church and State depended on educated clerks in holy orders. The monastery schools offered intelligent boys a way into the University as scholars; a degree would enable them to become teachers or to aspire to comfortable church livings or well-rewarded offices of State.

At Oxford the Masters' guild, known as *universitas*, was well established by the year 1200; it was confirmed by the Church in 1214 with the appointment of a Chancellor. Once the University was recognised, Oxford attracted an influx of scholars, many of them very young, who engendered some disorder and friction with the townspeople; this broke out from time to time in violent "town-and-gown" riots. The University owned no buildings before 1320 and was free to move; some of the riots caused migrations of Masters and scholars to other towns, including Cambridge where in 1209 they founded or enlarged the nucleus of another university.

Magdalen College tower carving

Hertford College's "Bridge of Sighs"

Corpus Christi College, The Radcliffe Camera and
St. Mary's Church over The Thames at Christ Church Meadows

Winter

The Masters began in the 13th century to gather the young scholars into halls of residence where they might have adequate living quarters and protection from a hostile town, and would be subject to some discipline. Eventually a certain amount of teaching was done in the halls and some of them gained a good reputation, but they were impermanent since each depended on the enterprise of a Master who in turn had to obtain the approval of the guild. Academic halls came and

went; the names of some two hundred have been recorded, though probably not more than eighty existed at any one time in the 13th and 14th centuries.

By the beginning of the 15th century the halls had academic status, and in 1420 a Royal Statute decreed that students would be admitted to the University only when they were matriculated (enrolled) at a recognised Academic Hall or College.

The first endowed colleges appeared at the same time as the halls, in the 13th century, but their origins and aims were different. The secular priests who had become rich churchmen and ministers of the Crown were under Church rules celibate, and had no openly recognised progeny to inherit their wealth. A commendable act was to found and endow a college, primarily for "Founder's Kin", to prepare priests for rewarding places in Church and State, and for scholars to pray for the Founder's soul.

The first colleges in Oxford – up to the Reformation – were not in competition with the halls, but they were a secular reply to the monasteries, with their secure buildings, good living, and internal discipline; besides this the colleges could encourage more adventurous thinking than was normal in a monastery. That was important, and the founders of two colleges expressly forbade their members to make any monastic vow.

Though not in calculated competition with the halls, the colleges' financial resources, ownership of their buildings, and above all their permanence, with statutes and elected Fellows, meant that they were able to do more effectively everything that the halls did, especially from the 15th century when scholars as well as Masters were lodged and boarded all under one roof. The medieval halls slowly disappeared; with one exception they were either closed or bought and absorbed by their rich college neighbours.

The first three colleges were founded within a few years of each other in the 13th century: University College ("Univ"), Merton, and Balliol. The question of which is the oldest rests on the definition of foundation: the

Books chained to the shelves in Merton College Library, and, below, a view of the garden at Rhodes House

Brasenose College Front Quad and The Radcliffe Camera

endowment; the ownership of permanent buildings; or the royal approval of statutes. However, St Edmund Hall, the sole survivor of the medieval halls, can claim to be the oldest teaching establishment, already in existence half a century before the first three colleges.

Four colleges were set up in the 14th century: Exeter, Oriel, Queen's, and New College. The founder of this last, William of Wykeham, set a pattern for college life when he stipulated that scholars should live in college and be taught by resident Masters, who would cover the whole university curriculum in the Faculty of Arts – that is, for a Master's degree. The practice of scholars living in college and "reading with a Master" became general.

In the 15th century three colleges were founded by rich prelates: Lincoln, All Souls, and Magdalen. They were set up on medieval lines, the members being enjoined to pray for the Founder's soul and to prepare themselves to defend the Faith and combat heresy. Two more colleges were founded early in the 16th century before the Reformation: Brasenose and Corpus Christi.

The 16th century is remarkable for the founding of Christ Church by King Henry VIII in 1546, despite the upheaval of the Reformation. He completed part of the great college conceived by Cardinal Wolsey, and thereby gave his approval to the University, which some "greedy souls" would have dissolved for its revenues.

The Dissolution of the Monasteries had the effect of cutting off Oxford's supply of young monastic scholars; however, from the Elizabethan age the rising middle classes increasingly demanded a university education for their sons, and were willing to pay for it; the colleges were glad to accept the fees, and the "gentleman commoner", who was not a member of the foundation but more like a paying guest, crowded out the tonsured indigent scholar.

After the Reformation and the founding of Christ Church three colleges were set up in the 16th century: Trinity, St John's, and Jesus, bringing the total to thirteen.

The rather rapid expansion of the colleges, each with its group of buildings, was not accompanied by a parallel material growth of the University. From its beginnings in the 12th century for more than a hundred years the Masters' guild owned no building; important ceremonials, ecclesiastical trials, and even the day-to-day business of the Masters – including making loans to scholars from the University Chest – all were conducted in the nave of St Mary the Virgin, known as the University Church. The modest Congregation House built in 1320 adjoining the north-east corner of the church provided a sort of committee room for the Masters, with an upper floor for the incipient library, but for major events they still used the church, and the University had no visible material presence.

Encaenia Procession

Christ Church Hall

Similarly the teaching side had no lecture-halls of its own until a century later, when about 1420 the Masters began to build proper lecture-rooms to replace the inadequate medieval hovels that were still being used. These early "schools" (faculty) buildings, standing where the Old Schools Quadrangle is today, were the first visible expression of the University in a town that already had several impressive college buildings.

The 16th century saw no university building until 1598 when Sir Thomas Bodley began the restoration of Duke Humfrey's Library – part of the 1420 buildings – and eventually the rebuilding of the schools quadrangle with three floors, the topmost storey being reserved for the rapidly growing library.

The expansive character of the Elizabethan age saw a great increase in academic activity and a rapid broadening of the fields of learning. This continued under James I; the University basked in his patronage, and Jacobean architecture sprang up all over Oxford. Two colleges were founded: Wadham and Pembroke; and in 1624 Sir Thomas Bodley's great library scheme was completed.

With Charles I on the throne, William Laud – successively Fellow and President of St John's, Chancellor of the University, confidant of the King, and Archbishop of Canterbury – drafted a new Statute for the University, known as the Caroline or Laudian Code of 1636; it created some resentment but it effectively regulated the University for many years.

During the Civil War the occupation of Oxford by the King, his Court, his army, and all the hangers-on, brought academic activity virtually to a standstill; many of the Fellows and most of the students disappeared. The colleges, in their royalist fervour, contributed loans to the King's exchequer – never repaid – and handed over much of their enormously valuable silver to be melted down for coinage.

The rule of the Commonwealth, though bitterly resented by staunch Royalists, brought about a revival of academic activity. Oliver Cromwell

Top: Stone carving on New College
Bottom: Glass in University College Chapel

Duke Humfrey's Library after the restoration in 1999

was Chancellor in 1650–57; as a Cambridge graduate he took Oxford's needs seriously, and the Parliamentarian appointments to vacated fellowships were acknowledged, even by Royalists, to be good scholars.

The Restoration revived Oxford's confidence, and Archbishop Gilbert Sheldon, a former Warden of All Souls and later Chancellor, commissioned another All Souls man, Christopher Wren, to design an assembly hall for the ceremonials and sometimes rowdy celebrations that were still being most unsuitably held at St Mary's Church. The Sheldonian Theatre, opened in 1669 was the University's second major building, and it has lost none of its importance over the years.

The 17th century also saw great building activity among the colleges and the emergence of two talented amateur architects: Henry Aldrich, Dean of Christ Church, and George Clarke, Fellow of All Souls, who both, with advice from the professionals such as Wren and Hawksmoor, greatly enriched Oxford architecturally.

The University maintained its sense of importance during the 18th century and was able to add majestically to its material presence with the Clarendon Building and the Radcliffe Camera. The trustees of Dr John Radcliffe's estate also gave Oxford the Radcliffe Infirmary (1770) and the Radcliffe Observatory (1794) with its beautiful Tower of Winds.

These additions to the University's material presence may have stimulated the science faculties but they did little for the Arts, where academic standards were low. The prevailing indolence also affected religious observance, and this deeply offended John and Charles Wesley, both graduates of Christ Church, who in 1729 with some equally indignant friends formed the Holy Club to encourage the primitive spirit of Christianity, and they some years later laid the foundations of the Methodist Church.

Only two colleges were founded in the 18th century – more correctly, refounded, since both had ancient antecedents and some buildings – namely Worcester and Hertford. Building work also went on at All Souls, Queen's, Magdalen, and the Radcliffe Camera.

The 19th century brought in radical reforms and far-reaching changes in university life. When college Fellows were no longer obliged to be in holy orders, were free to marry, and were required to undertake serious teaching or research, men of a different calibre were attracted to university work; the colleges began to elect Fellows for their intellectual capacity rather than for their capacity for port wine, and there were soon erudite men in the colleges.

By the 1870s university life was respectable and interesting and the teaching was serious. The scene was set for the greatest revolution in the University's history: the admission of women. Between 1878 and 1898 four colleges for women and the Society of Home Students (later St Anne's) were founded; resistance to the advent of women delayed until 1920 their right to receive degrees, and the women's halls – as they technically were – did not acquire full college status until 1959.

The 19th century was remarkably expansive; besides the women's colleges, several major university buildings were put up, including the new Examination Schools in the High Street, the University Press building in Walton Street, the Ashmolean Museum in Beaumont Street, and the University Museum in Parks Road. Virtually all the existing colleges were enlarged, and Keble College was founded and built.

Fourteen new colleges have been established in the 20th century; seven of these already existed in another form and have now achieved independent college status. The logical, even inevitable, outcome of the 19th-century decision to admit women to the University has been the 20th-century admission of women to the men's colleges, and then of men to the women's.

In the 21st century, Oxford's research aims to address some of the major challenges facing humanity in modern times. Global health is one aspect of this work: with one of the largest medical research centres in Europe, Oxford runs world-leading programmes on cancer, stroke, malaria, HIV, heart disease, and musculoskeletal and neurological disorders. The Oxford Martin School, set up in 2005, carries out interdisciplinary research into global issues ranging from climate change to the ageing population of the developed world. The University has also extended the range of its teaching, with the new Blavatnik School of Government set to train future world leaders.

The ongoing development of scientific research has been matched by the provision of improved facilities, with major new buildings in the Science Area. The University's purchase of the Radcliffe Infirmary site has also enabled the creation of a new central campus, the Radcliffe Observatory Quarter. The first buildings planned for the site are for mathematics and the humanities, with further development expected to take place over several decades. The University's extensive library system, managed by the Bodleian Libraries, is being modernised, bringing improvements in access, efficiency and conservation standards, not least through the refurbishment of the New Bodleian Library, due to reopen as the Weston Library, and through major digitisation projects. The University's museums have also focused on improving research facilities and public access, with major extensions at the Pitt Rivers Museum and at the Ashmolean Museum, which has doubled its exhibition space with an award-winning redesign.

One new college, Green Templeton College, was founded in 2008 following the merger of Green College and Templeton College. Other colleges have continued to extend their facilities through conversions and new buildings.

THE DREAMING SPIRES

Central Oxford from Trinity College Tower

Central Oxford over the Great Quad, New College

Oxford from Boars Hill

The City from South Hinksey

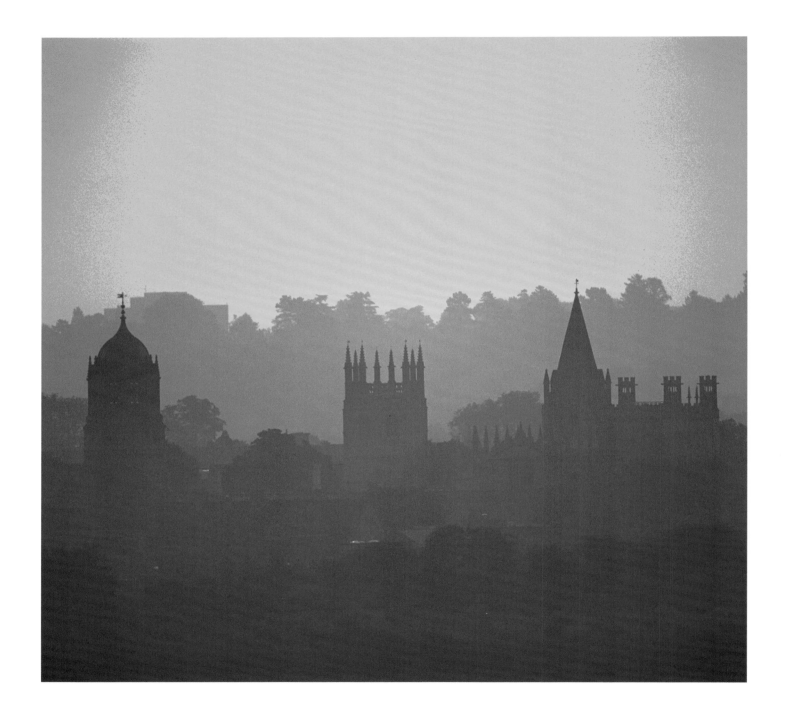

Sunrise, Christ Church and Merton College

Early morning, central Oxford from the north

Christ Church, Corpus Christi and Merton Colleges

Christ Church, Merton College and Oxford

Oxford from the west at sunrise

The City from the east in winter

THE COLLEGES

All Souls College

All Souls towers are by Dr George Clarke, Warden of the College, and
Nicholas Hawksmoor, dating from 1714-34

Balliol College Chapel and Front Quad

Front Quad and gate-tower, though Balliol is one of the three oldest Oxford Colleges, these buildings are 19th century

Balliol College Hall

The Fellows' Garden with "Dervorguilla's tomb"

*Brasenose College High Street front
with St. Mary's Church*

*Opposite: The College gateway in
Radcliffe Square*

Christ Church Cathedral and Tom Quad,
with Mercury Fountain

Tom Tower and the gatehouse built in 1682 by Christopher Wren, housing the bell "Great Tom"

Christ Church Hall, Alden Cottage
and The Memorial Gardens

Cleaning the windows of the Library

Corpus Christi College. The Pelican is taken from the founder's coat of arms and symbolizes the Body of Christ

Fellows' Garden (and gardeners)

Exeter College Chapel, the College is the fourth oldest,
founded in 1314 by the Bishop of Exeter

The Library and Fellows' Garden

*Inside the Radcliffe Observatory, the building is
now part of Green Templeton College*

Hertford College stair tower

*Hertford College Front Quad and Stair Tower, like most of the
College built by the architect Thomas Jackson*

Two parts of the College are joined by one of Oxford's most recognised landmarks, the "Bridge of Sighs"

Jesus College First Quad and entrance

*Inner Quad, with spectacular borders
and wysteria in season*

Jesus College and Turl Street

Keble College and Parks Road

Keble Chapel and College buildings with
Oxford from the north

*Lady Margaret Hall, the first college
specifically set up for women members*

Lady Margaret Hall's garden compliments its
attractive riverside setting

Linacre College, one of the more recent foundations,
acquired full collegiate status in 1986

Lincoln College, the 15th century Front Quad

The church of All Saints, now the College library

Magdalen College, the New Buildings and Spring flowers

The meadow in Addison's Walk with its
wonderful display of fritillaries

Magdalen sits on a branch of the Cherwell and has
many beautiful riverside walks and views

The Grove has contained deer since the late 17th century

Overleaf: Magdalen College and Oxford from the east

Mansfield College

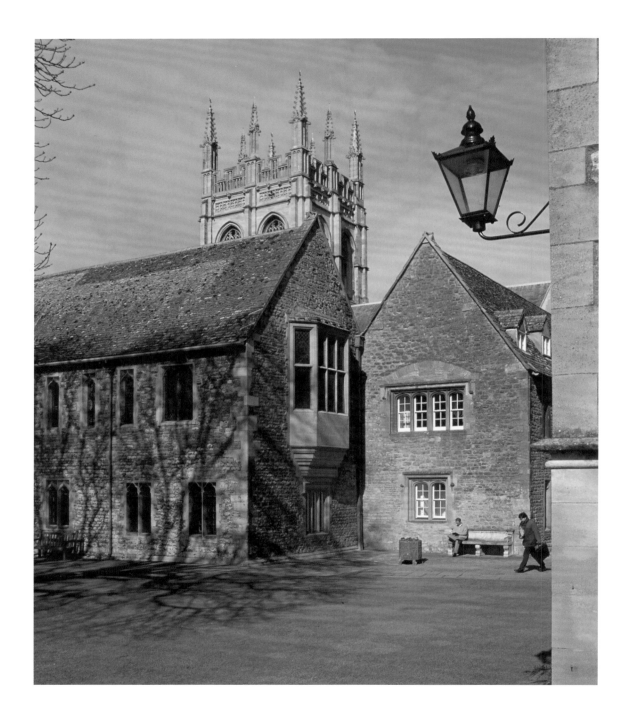

Merton, one of the three oldest Oxford Colleges

The Chapel Tower and the Meadow aspect
of the College

Merton and Oxford from the south with the Old City Wall

The College gardens

New College Great Quad and Oxford
from the College Tower

Garden Quad and grounds

A view of the Holywell Street buildings,
and a part of the Old City Wall

The later buildings of Garden Quad house the earliest
recorded examples of sash windows in Oxford

Nuffield College and the Oxford Canal

Oriel College, the entrance to the Hall with statues of Edward II and Charles I, with Queen Mary above and early diners below

Oriel College Front Quad

Inside the 1788 Palladian library

Pembroke College, founded by two men from Abingdon,
initially to cater for scholars from Abingdon School

The Hall

*The Queen's College High Street front, with the
statue of Queen Caroline*

The Hall and Chapel in Front Quad

St Anne's College

The College gardens

St Cross College

St Catherine's College, built to a design by the
Danish architect, Arne Jacobson

College Tower and Quad

St Edmund Hall and Oxford

Front Quad with buildings from the 16th century

St Hilda's College and the River Cherwell

The gardens and College punts

St Hugh's College, the iron gates at the
entrance to the Principal's Lodgings

Gardens with Magnolia and the main buildings

St John's College, the main entrance and
frontage on St Giles'

*The outer face of Canterbury Quad with a sculpture
exhibition on the lawn*

Garden Quad, completed in 1996

The garden

Trinity and St John's Colleges, with St Giles'
The Ashmolean Museum and St Cross College

Somerville College Front Quad

The Library and gardens

Trinity College from Parks Road

Trinity College Garden Quad and lawns, the buildings
originally by Christopher Wren, but with later additions

Trinity College Chapel and gatehouse,
the original main entrance

The Hall set for a formal dinner

*University College Front Quad, "Univ" is one of
the three oldest Oxford Colleges*

The Master's Lodgings and Radcliffe Quad

Fan vaulting in Radcliffe Quad archway

The memorial to Shelley, who was an
undergraduate at "Univ"

Wadham College, the original foundation one of Oxford's most harmonious,
having been built under one person, and in only three years 1610-1613

Looking towards the new Bowra Building with bluebells
carpeting the ground outside the Chapel

Wadham College Front Quad

Wolfson College, on the banks of the Cherwell

Worcester College, medieval cottages in Front Quad

Library and Front Quad

Worcester is the only Oxford College to have its own lake,
seen here in early autumn

The College cricket pavilion in winter

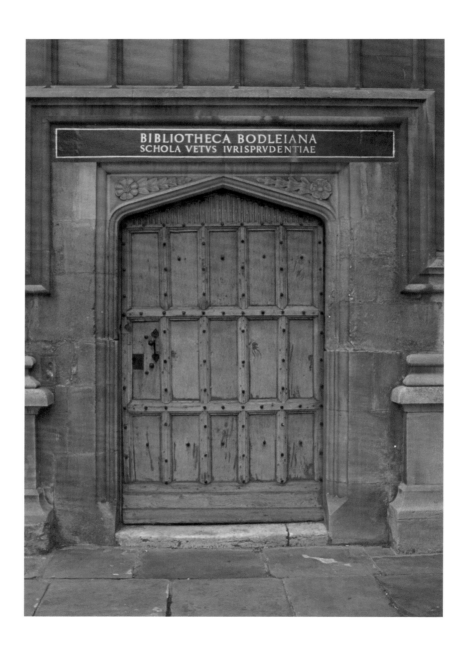

Doorway in The Old Schools Quad

St Mary's Church, The Radcliffe Camera, Old and New Bodleian Library, The Sheldonian Theatre
with details of Oriel, All Souls, Trinity, Exeter and Brasenose Colleges

The Bodleian Library Old Schools Quad frontispiece

*St Mary's Church and The Radcliffe Camera with the east
face of The Bodleian Library*

123

Botanic Garden gateway

Fountain in the Garden in summer

The Radcliffe Camera

Radcliffe Square on an autumnal morning

The Sheldonian Theatre and The Clarendon Building

The Oxford University Press

The University Church of St Mary The Virgin

The Ashmolean Museum

The Saïd Business School of 2001

College boathouses and the Thames

OXFORD LIFE

Oriel College junior regatta on the
Thames at Port Meadow

May Ball at St Hugh's College

Historians in Balliol College

Jesus College ladies hockey team

Snowballs in Magdalen College

Blackwell's bookshop

Freshers welcome party at St Anne's College

At the Examination Schools

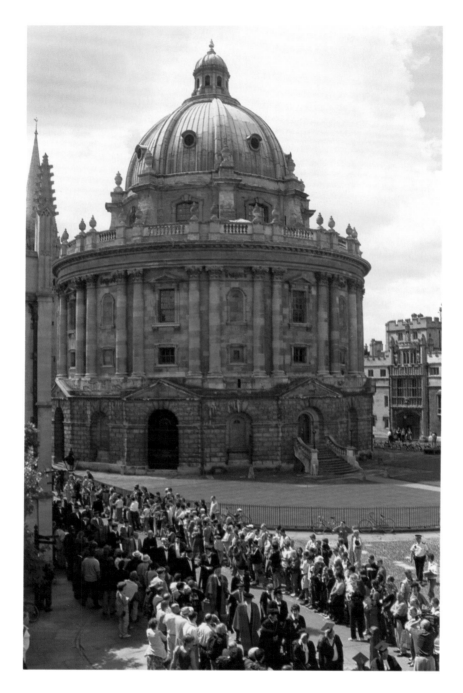

The Radcliffe Camera and
Encaenia Procession

And that sweet city with her dreaming spires,
She needs not June for beauty's heightening,

MATTHEW ARNOLD

INDEX